The
Strategy Concepts
of
Bill Belichick

A Leadership Case Study of the New England Patriots Head Coach

\

Additional Leadership Case Studies

The Management Ideas of Nick Saban

The Turnaround Strategies of Jim Harbaugh

The Motivational Techniques of Urban Meyer

The Leadership Lessons of Gregg Popovich

The Work Ethic of Tom Brady, Peyton Manning, and Aaron Rodgers

The Team Building Strategies of Steve Kerr

Table of Contents

Introduction

How does he do it? How does New England Patriots head coach Bill Belichick lead his organization to the playoffs on a yearly basis? In a competitive industry where the rules are designed to create parity, how is it that one team can remain competitive for over a decade?

Since he took over the New England Patriots at the turn of the century, Bill Belichick has been one of best coaches in the National Football League. During his tenure, he has won 4 Super Bowls, tied for the most Super Bowl wins as a head coach for all time. He has been named the Associated Press Head Coach of the year 3 times. He has the most playoffs wins as a head coach in history. In a highly competitive industry where turnover is high, Belichick is currently the longest active coach to be with the same team.

In this Leadership Case Study, we analyze the management ideas and concepts of Bill Belichick. We focus on the strategies that he employs to create an organization that has won 4 Super Bowl Championships and outperforms his competition.

Part 1 covers the CULTURE of the New England Patriots. The phrase "Do Your Job" is used by Belichick to get everyone on the team to perform at a high level. We discuss Belichick's views on leadership, and how he communicates his message to his entire team.

Part 2 analyzes the PREPARATION and work ethic of Bill Belichick. The New England Patriots are always considered to be one of the most disciplined and prepared team in the NFL. How do they learn? How does Bill Belichick prepare his team to be ready for any situation?

Part 3 of this case study highlights the PERFORMANCE aspect of Bill Belichick's strategic mind. Belichick is able to get his team to focus on the task at hand and to eliminate the distractions that impact on-field performances. Along with the incredible focus, we highlight the adaptability of Belichick's strategy to exploit opponent's weaknesses.

The lessons that can be learned from Bill Belichick are not simply about football. Although we use a few situations that took place on the football field, the strategic ideas of Bill Belichick can be applied to any aspect of your life. Whether you are a manager, a consultant, or simply looking to gain a competitive advantage in life, then the ideas of Belichick can be helpful to you.

To help apply the lessons from this case study, there are a few review questions listed after each section to help apply them to your own business or program.

All information in this case study has been collected from public sources. Links to the articles, videos and documents are available at our website leadershipcasestudies.com.

Background Information About Bill Belichick

Date of Birth: April 16, 1952

College Education: Bachelor's Degree in Economics, Wesleyan University, 1975.

Head Coaching Experience:

Cleveland Browns (1991-1995)

New England Patriots (2000-Present)

Super Bowl Championships as Head Coach:

New England Patriots (2001, 2003, 2004, 2014)

Super Bowl Record as Head Coach: 4 wins, 2 losses.

Associated Press Coach of the Year:
2003, 2007, 2010

Part 1: Culture

Do Your Job

One of the key terms that is associated with Bill Belichick and the New England Patriots is "Do your job." This saying is ingrained into all of the players, staff and coaches. In fact, after winning the 2015 Super Bowl, the phrase "Do Your Job" was inscribed on the championship rings.

Although the phrase seems to be pretty straightforward, Bill Belichick and his players put a lot of thought into the phrase. To them, the phrase serves as a mission statement in how to conduct their business. It can be adjusted and applied to many different situations and brings everyone in the organization together in their purpose.

"I think in terms of our players and our team, each of us has a job to do, and the only thing that we can do is do the best that we can," Belichick stated when asked about the phrase. By doing the best in everything that they do, each player and staff member is striving towards the goals of the larger organization.

The goal laid out by Belichick isn't an external goal, such as winning championships or achieving a certain win total. Rather, the goal is to "improve on a daily basis, work hard, pay attention to the little details and put the team first."

These goals of improving everyday and putting in the effort is solely in control of the team members. Everyone can meet their goals on a daily basis. There is no external factor or excuse that can prevent a player from working hard, paying attention, and striving to get better. Belichick makes sure that the goals set out are achievable by the player, and are not based on other factors.

"So whether it's myself, a player or an assistant coach, it doesn't really matter who it is, we all can only do what we can do. And we try to do that in team context, and try to work as hard at it as we can and improve on a daily basis," Belichick says.

Individual Performance

Despite being a team and a large organization, Belichick believes that individuals still have to execute at their own specific roles. There is a balance between focusing on the organization and having an individual perform at a high level.

While giving a keynote address entitled "Building a champion", Belichick explained his thought process about individual performance. "We've all heard the saying 'there's no I in team' but in my mind I think there is a balance on that. There is an 'I' in 'win' and that stands for individual performance," he says in a transcript compiled by ESPN Boston. "We can all stand around in the locker room and hold hands and chant 'Team! Team! Team!' all day and that isn't going to do anything. We have to go out there and individually perform. There is a balance there."

According to Belichick, an emphasis on individual performance in a team setting creates a feedback loop that raises the performance of the entire team. When everyone is focused on their own job, then each player is able to take comfort knowing that the person next to them is doing their job as well. Without having to worry about the next person, each individual player is able to put their complete focus, dedication, and effort into their own task, which raises the performance of the entire team.

By "being solid and doing your job, and if you're prepared and everybody around you knows that you are prepared and they can count on you, and you're dependable to go out and do your job, then it makes it a lot easier for the person beside you to go out and do theirs," he says.

"So if I'm playing right tackle and if I know the right guard is prepared - he's studied, he's dependable, he's going to do everything he can to do the right thing, well, I'm just going out there and doing my job," Belichick states. "I'm not thinking about whether he's going to be here, or be there, and if we call this is he going to get it or not get it?"

As Belichick puts it, when one person does their job, "the next person can go out there and do their job without really a lot of concern about what's going to happen around them. They're confident of their teammate and the guy beside them."

This concept of doing your own job well leads all the way up to the head coach. Belichick understands fully that his job is create the game plan that will give his team the best opportunity to win.

"I think that extends to the entire organization as the head coach, that I want to go out there and try to be focused on the job that I have to do," Belichick says. "I can't make medical decisions. I can't block. I can't kick. I can't throw. That's not my job. Other people we have doing their jobs, I don't think we want them doing mine. So it can all work together as long as we understand our role."

Leadership

A key role in any organization is that of the leader. Belichick believes that the only way a player can be a leader on the team is by performing their own job at a high level. No one will be willing to follow someone who isn't competent at their own job.

"If you don't do your job, I don't see how you can give any leadership. A lot of people who aren't very good at doing their job, and who try to give leadership, are just looked at as 'Look buddy, why don't you just do your job? Why don't we start with that instead of trying to tell everybody else what to do?'"

In addition to performing their jobs at a high level, Belichick believes that there are many types of leadership styles. Belichick doesn't fall into the trap of thinking that a leader is the most vocal person on the team, or someone who gives a great speech.

"I can say through almost 40 years of NFL experience that leadership comes in a lot of shapes and sizes. I've had players who were very vocal that were great leaders. I've had players who were vocal that weren't great leaders. We've had other players that would never say a word."

Belichick uses the example of Troy Brown as a great example of a leader on a team. Brown wasn't the most vocal of the players, but he would do his job and would always put the interests of the team first. "When Troy Brown played for us, he returned kicks, he covered kicks, he caught a lot of passes in the slot, he blocked and when we needed him in some very critical situations he went over and played defense against some very good teams and very good players."

It's important to note that Belichick again emphasizes that "do your job" doesn't mean achieving a specific result, but rather involves doing the best that the person can do. When speaking about Troy Brown doing whatever was asked by the coaches, Belichick says "Was it always perfect? No, but he competed as hard as he could. He did the very best he could for the team and that's all you could ask for; it didn't matter what it was."

"Here is an example of a guy who was as good of a leader as I've ever coached who said probably less than any player of his stature that I've ever coached. So it's not about volume or who's the most talkative guy. It's the guy who does his job and puts the best interests of the team and organization in the lead."

Communication

As the leader of a large organization, Belichick faces the same problems that managers face around the world: being able to communicate with the entire organization. "One of the things that I deal with, and I'm sure many of you do too, is just a volume of people," he says. "It's impossible to deal with every one of those guys on an individual basis on a daily basis. You pick your spots with guys here and there, but you still have to connect with the whole team."

Like any CEO in Corporate America, Belichick relies upon managers and department heads to keep him informed. In the NFL, that role is given to the team captains. "As it relates to whatever organization you have, you have other people responsible for other people below you, and I've always felt that having the right people as captains was critical."

The captains represent the team in meetings with the coaching staff, and are used by Belichick to get his message across the entire organization. By having strong leaders who are able to set an example and communicate clearly, the team is able to quickly and efficiently communicate its ideas throughout the program.

"They represent everybody - the offense, the defense, special teams, linemen, skill groups, and there are a couple guys on the younger side, a couple guys on the older side," Belichick says of his captains. The group is able to represent the many interests of the team and represents the diversity of a large organization.

"It's a good way for me to get a good pulse of the team but also to hear their message, and in some cases, deliver my message to them because it's going to carry some weight when it comes from them," Belichick says of his captains. "Once those guys are in those positions, they're not just out there to walk out there for the toss of the coin; that's really the least of their responsibilities. Their job really comes more to setting an example, showing leadership, and most importantly communicating one way or the other - whether its from the players to me or from me to the players - what we need to get done."

Belichick continues, "It's hard when you have a large group of people, and all of them have their own individual interests, that you collectively have to try to bring everyone together to see it through, as much as you can, one set of eyes - one vision- is challenging on a lot of levels."

To meet this challenge, Belichick strives to make sure that the right people are in the right positions. The players on the team vote for the team captains, and Belichick says that most of the time, the team votes for the same person that Belichick would. If the team votes for a person that Belichick wouldn't have chosen, then that is a sign of a wider problem.

"I would say that when the team is not voting for the people that you'd think are the right people, then you probably have problems all the way through your team. If you don't have a good team, and they're voting guys into leadership positions, you know you have problems all the way through," he says.

When these types of issues come up, Belichick addresses it quickly. "Either you're going to make changes or they're going to change you - one or the other." This mindset of Belichick is one of the reasons why many players who join the Patriots quickly fall into line. Many former players who have had problems with other teams were able to adjust to the Patriots and to do their job. They were able to buy into the Patriots' culture due to Belichick addressing any problems quickly, and allowing his captains to lead by example. The focus on doing your job is reinforced by the players, staff, and Belichick himself.

Accepting Responsibility

Another method that Belichick uses to get everyone to do their job is to hold people accountable for their actions. Although the team captains and veteran leadership preserve the culture in the locker room, in the end the coaching staff must be the final judge of the players.

Belichick views self-evaluation and holding each player accountable as a key part of his coaching strategy. "The only way for us as a team to get a championship level is to continue to evaluate ourselves, and we have to look at what we've done and critically analyze it," he says.

Unlike other industries, NFL teams can not rely on outside experts to come into their team and help fix problems. Any type of accountability and improvements must be created internally. In a competitive industry like professional sports, a successful organization needs to be able to address its shortfalls on its own. "We can't hire a consultant to come in and fix our problems," Belichick says. "There is no team in the league that wants to help us and there's no team in the league that we want to help."

Thus, in order to remain competitive in a league where the rules are built for parity, the improvement must come from within. "So the only way for us to get better is to do our own R&D (research and development)." Belichick means that everyone in the organization must study, learn, and strive to get better.

To do that, everyone must have an open mindset and be willing to learn and be evaluated. That comes with "a certain amount of humility," he states, along with the ability to take "constructive criticism." "We certainly have all made a lot of mistakes. I've made more than my share and so has everybody else."

Understanding that mistakes are not fatal, and that only by addressing the problem can things improve, Belichick wants all of his players to feel that they don't have to be worried or scared about admitting mistakes.

"In order for us to improve and get better and move forward, we've all got to be able to stand up and say 'Hey, I screwed that up' or 'I didn't do a good job here, how can we correct the problem and get it right the next time?'", he says. This trait of accepting responsibility is one that Belichick feels is very important in his organization. "In our society, I would say there is not an over-abundance of that out there. There's a lot more trying to point the finger at somebody else and make excuses, and all that. So we try to eliminate that in our organization."

Review Questions

1. How clear are the roles in your organization? Does everyone know what their jobs and responsibilities are? If you wrote down what you thought your player's role was, and he wrote down what he thought his role was, how close would the two statements be? What about with other members of your team? Are you intruding on another person's responsibilities? Is someone trying to do your job? What about in your personal life? Do you understand how your family or friends view your responsibilities? Are you meeting their expectations?

2. How do you view the leaders in your organization? How do you select or promote people? Do you think that the person who is the most vocal is the best leader? Could you be missing something in your team because it isn't the most vocal or gets the most attention? Could there be people in your life that could do more positive things if you noticed them?

3. Do you allow people in your organization to fail? Are your players or workers so afraid of failure that they never attempt to do something new? Do you criticize or embarrass anyone who makes a mistake, or do you help them learn from it? What about yourself? When was the last time you tried something and failed? Are you taking enough calculated risks? Do you beat yourself up after you make a mistake? Or do you tell yourself that mistakes are a part of life and then try to learn from the mistake?

Part 2: Preparation

Strong Foundation

In order to understand his industry, Belichick is able to draw upon a wide range of knowledge. Due to his immense knowledge of the game, Belichick is widely considered to be one of the smartest football coaches.

Bill Belichick father was also a football coach and collected an extensive library of football books. The oldest book in the collection is *American Football by Walter Camp*, which was written in 1891. Steve Belichick collected these books while traveling across the country on scouting trips, while other books were given to him by friends in the coaching industry.

As the website Monday Morning Quarterback (MMQB) writes, "There may not be a collection like this anywhere else in the world." The book collection is packed with so many unique football books that it is now housed at the Naval Academy, where Steve Belichick was a longtime coach.

These four hundred and thirteen books served as the foundation of Bill Belichick's football knowledge. It is highly unlikely that any other coach in the NFL has the breadth and scope of football history, strategy, and techniques as Bill Belichick.

Based upon all of the books that Belichick has read, one does stand out. Charles Robinson of Yahoo Sports writes that "To this day, Belichick insists *Bill Walsh: Finding the Winning Edge* is the greatest piece of football literature regarding a franchise blueprint ever written. Belichick read the book in the nuclear winter of his own coaching career, between the disaster with the Cleveland Browns and resurrection with the New England Patriots. At a time in his lifetime when Belichick was forced to re-examine his basic truths about team building, he wrapped his hands around the second of several books by Walsh."

"When he was finished, Belichick's philosophical foundation as a coach had once again solidified beneath his feet."

Finding New Advantages and Information

With his extensive knowledge of football history and strategy, Bill Belichick has a great foundation to build upon it. He is constantly adding to his expertise by finding new information and ideas to win football games. He doesn't care where the ideas come from, or who offers the ideas. For example, during staff meetings with his coaches, he first asks his staff for their ideas and suggestions. The reason that he remains silent during the opening minutes of a strategy session is that he doesn't want to limit or influence the ideas of his staff. He knows that if he offers his own suggestions first, then his coaches may knowingly or unknowingly be inclined to follow his suggestions.

Belichick is on a constant quest to learn, even after winning a Super Bowl. Gil Brandt served as the personnel director of the Dallas Cowboys during the Tom Landry years. He told USA Today that he received a phone call from Belichick asking for information. What was so startling to Brandt was that Belichick was calling on the way home from the White House, where his team was just honored for winning the Super Bow. "As accomplished as he is, that's the beauty of Belichick's edge," writes Jarrett Bell in the article. "He's not so full of himself that he won't listen, and won't tap into any source for an edge."

Another way that Belichick finds ways to be competitive is through his extensive use of analytics. Belichick was one of the first coaches in the NFL to fully embrace analytics and the use of advanced statistics in his coaching. In fact, he was awarded the Lifetime Achievement Award by the Sloan Sports Analytics Conference in 2013.

In his taped acceptance speech, Belichick stated that he is open to using any method in finding an advantage. This constant search for new information lead him to analytics. "I certainly respect the mathematical and statistical ways of looking at the game, looking at football, and try to use those methods and those results to improve our product on the field," he said.

"The analytics and different ways of trying to improve and construct a team are important, and we're all here to do one thing - whatever our role or job, whatever team or organization we work for - and that's to try to find ways to improve, to find a better way to approach our team or business, to look at different strategies, and to pick the best one and ultimately try to motivate and instruct the people that we work with to perform to a higher level, including ourselves."

Work Ethic

The work ethic of Bill Belichick is legendary, even when compared to other workaholics in the NFL. Jeff Howe of NESN writes that Patriots players have seen Belichick working at all hours of the day.

"Some Patriots report to Gillette Stadium as early as 5:30 in the morning. Other will watch film at the facility until midnight or 1 a.m. Belichick, everyone of them says, has been in the building at each end of that spectrum. They know there are nights when Belichick sleeps at Gillette, and some Patriots have wondered - seriously, jokingly, whatever - if he ever leaves."

"When everyone else is sleeping, or tweeting, or playing Madden, or lounging around, Belichick is studying the game, whether it's that week's opponent or one of his old playoff itineraries," writes Howe. "He is always working to implement improvements for the good of his team's success, and he's always been willing to adjust something he thought he once screwed up."

Based on his preparation and studying, Belichick has an enormous amount of information at his disposal. With this knowledge, he is able to exploit any advantage that he can find. When he finds these advantages, Belichick expects his players to know then as well.

Teaching Players

One method that Belichick teaches his players is through the use of daily quizzes. Belichick makes sure that every player is actively paying attention during the week by keeping them on their toes. According to the Wall Street Journal, "they must be ready, at any moment, for the NFL's version of Alex Trebek: The quiz master Belichick."

Current and former players all say that "no one commands a depth of knowledge quite like Belichick, who has a habit of blurting out obscure yet crucial questions. These typically come in midweek meetings, but they can happen anywhere in the team facility on any day."

Former Patriots player and current NFL Network analyst Heath Evans told the Wall Street Journal that he hated walking by Belichick on a Thursday if he was unprepared. "There's no limit to the knowledge Bill expects you to have on an opponent and the craziest part is he has the answers to all of it," Evans said.

Here is just a small sample of the types of questions Belichick expects his players to know.

- How does a player on special teams perform? Who did he match up against last week on kickoffs and how did he win that matchup?
- When did an opposing player join the team? What is his background?
- The Patriots are in the red zone, it's second-and-six from the 18. What is Indianapolis' favorite blitz to run in this situation?

Everyone is expected to study, regardless of their role on the team and how much playing time they are expected to have. For example, McLeod Bethel-Thompson was a practice squad quarterback who was with the team from August 31 to September 9 during the 2014 season. Despite this short time he was with the team, Belichick grilled Bethel-Thompson and expected him to know the game plan.

The role of a practice squad quarterback is to imitate the opposing quarterback to help the Patriots defense prepare for the game. Belichick is very interested in the opposing quarterback's psychology, and expected Bethel-Thompson to put in the time to study.

"He'd challenge you - why'd you make that throw? Why'd you attack [Patriots cornerback Darrelle] Revis - would the opposing quarterback challenge Revis?," Bethel-Thompson told the Wall Street Journal. He said that Belichick wanted to know specific details and focused in on the things that the role of a practice squad quarterback should know.

Kyle Arrington, a cornerback on the Super Bowl winning team, sounded like a political operative digging up dirt on an opposing candidate when asked how Belichick forces them to prepare. "You just have to Wikipedia, Google, SportsCenter, use your ESPN app, something," Arrington said. "You do what you've got to do."

These quizzes and intense preparation clearly pays off for the players on game day. Safety Patrick Chung says that these quizzes and Belichick's accountability prepares the players to play fast on Sundays. "It keeps our minds going, it's a daily thing," Chung says. "If you can anticipate certain things, or you know the game plan inside out, it makes it a lot easier to play fast. If you're thinking about stuff, it's impossible to play fast."

For players who are unable to keep up, Belichick will quickly weed them out. "Everything he does to train the mind of the athlete is perfect," Heath Evans raves about Belichick. "When guys get there they either buy in immediately or they are so overwhelmed that they want out."

Importance of Practice

These examples are just a portion of the methods that Belichick uses to improve his team. Belichick believes that the team has to be improving all the time in order to compete in the NFL. And the only way to improve is through practice.

"Practice is a very important part of our development," he stated. "You look at a lot of the other sports - baseball, basketball, hockey and pro sports like that - those teams are playing daily and in some cases multiple times a week. We don't have that opportunity. We just play once a week."

With only 16 games during the regular season, a team cannot rely on game situations to improve. There simply isn't enough opportunities to correct mistakes and improve on an individual performance. "If we only improve on the days we play, we're not going to get very far. We have to improve on those other six days that we're not playing. Those are important days for our football team, and for our individual personal development, and the overall development of our team," Belichick said.

Through practice, the team is able to grow together. When players are unable to practice, Belichick states that "the overall communication and execution of the team is certainly not what it would be if they were able to participate."

Payoff of Preparation

To see a perfect example of how taking the time to study and prepare can pay off, then look no further to the ending of Super Bowl 49. With the ball on the one-yard line, the Seattle Seahawks threw a pass play that was intercepted by the Patriots' Malcolm Butler.

The Seahawks coaching staff was vilified by the media for that play call. Regardless of whether it was the right call or not, one thing was very clear: The Patriots were ready for that situation. They were prepared for that SPECIFIC play, and practiced defending that play during practice. Thus, when the ball was in the air, Malcolm Butler was able to intercept the ball because he practiced that play earlier in the week. Butler, an undrafted free agent, was coached and prepared by Bill Belichick and told to be ready for that play.

Ryan Wilson of CBS Sports explains how Malcolm Butler was prepared by Belichick for that specific situation:

> "In the days leading up to the Super Bowl - and The Interception - the Patriots scout team ran the same pass play we saw from Seattle's offense late in the fourth quarter that made cornerback Malcolm Butler the unlikeliest of heroes.
>
> And Butler was beaten.
>
> "I was at practice, and the scout team ran the same exact play," Butler told Dan Patrick on Wednesday, via PFT.com. "And I got beat on it at practice because I gave ground... BIll Belichick, he came and said to me "Malcolm, you've gotta be on that."

"I knew they were going to throw it," Butler said shortly after the game. "Our defensive coordinator is real smart and with a goal line, three cornerback formation we knew they were going to throw the ball."

Think of the preparation that paid off for the Patriots. First, they studied the Seahawks. They knew that they Seahawks would want to run that specific play in that situation. Then, they had to practice defending against that play. After their own scout team ran the play and scored, the Patriots had to get better at defending it. So then they had to correct the mistake that a cornerback made in order to properly defend against that play. They fixed the mistakes they made in practice, and made sure that the mistakes wouldn't happen during the game. All these things needed to happen in order for the Patriots to intercept the ball.

The preparation paid off, and helped the Patriots seal their victory in a Super Bowl.

Review Questions

1. What is your foundation? How well do you know your industry? Have you read all of the important books? Do you know all of the key terms in the field? Do you know the basics of your field, or are you just trying to learn as you go?

2. Where do you get new information from? Are you learning new things about your job? Are they the same sources as your competitors? Are you trying to learn new things that can give you an advantage? Belichick was one of the first in the NFL to use advanced statistics and analytics. What are the new tools and information that you can use to better yourself or your organization?

3. How are you teaching your team or organization? Is the message that you are trying to pass on to them really working? In addition to your own foundation, how is the foundation of your team? Does everyone know the basics? Do you need additional training? Do you even offer training and learning opportunities to your team?

Part 3: Performance

Focus

Throughout his tenure with the Patriots, Belichick has dealt with an intense media glare as he has been successful every year. By winning four Super Bowls and playing in six, the Patriots are always being discussed by the sports media.

Despite the media glare, the Patriots have been able to block out the noise and focus on the task at hand. Belichick has done an amazing job of eliminating the distractions and getting his players to focus on doing their job.

In their preview of the 2015 NFL season, Greg A. Bedard of the MMQB wrote that "No one navigates a minefield better than Belichick."

Bedard writes about some of the key issues and "minefields" that Belichick has dealt with during his time in New England:

"He overcame a quarterback controversy to win not just one Super Bowl, but three in four years. He has cut a defensive captain, traded a stalwart defensive lineman, jettisoned a Super Bowl MVP and had an All-Pro guard sit out eight games during a contract squabble; and he kept winning. Belichick has been fined by the league for taping the signals of opposing coaches, and he kept winning. He has lost a franchise quarterback in the season opener and turned to a guy who didn't start for his college team, and he kept winning. Belichick has even had a star player arrested and later convicted of first-degree murder, and the Patriots just kept winning," Bedard writes.

So how exactly does Belichick ignore the distractions? It's actually a pretty simple method. He simply declines to talk about anything that took place in the past and places the entire organization's focus on the next game. He doesn't try to correct the record, or attempt to justify his past actions. He simply moves on to the next issue and focuses on achieving his next goal.

The Patriots will be entering the 2015 season under great controversy due to Deflategate, but Bedard writes that Belichick will likely have his players ready and focused.

"They'll be instructed to not talk about the past, and they won't," he writes. "It's easier when the head coach is doing the same thing. And it's not a strategy that's just trotted out during moments of controversy. Even during the most mundane seasons, Belichick will refuse any interview that has to do with the past because he's solely focused on the next game. Want a few history lessons from arguably the greatest NFL coach ever? That will have to wait for a bye week, or the offseason."

There was a great example of this mindset during the 2014 Super Bowl winning season. In their fourth game of the season, the Patriots got smashed by the Kansas City Chiefs on Monday Night Football, losing by a score of 41-14. With that loss, the Patriots had a record of 2-2, and the judgements started raining down on them.

Monday Night Football analyst Trent Dilfer stated that they were simply not a good team. "We saw a weak team. The New England Patriots, let's face it, they're not good anymore. They're weak," Dilfer said after the game.

At his weekly press conference two days later, the media was focused on the team's record and began asking Belichick questions about the team. Instead of addressing the team troubles, Belichick instead kept the focus solely their next opponent, the Cincinnati Bengals.

Here is a transcript of the press conference provided by Boston.com that shows how Belichick will not let reporters create a distraction for his players.

Question: Your team has been successful for so long. How difficult is it to adjust to the adversity of Monday night's game and get back on track? This team and organization hasn't had these sort of issues in the past.

Belichick: We're on to Cincinnati.

Question: You mentioned Tom Brady's age at the draft -

Belichick: We're on to Cincinnati.

Question: Do you think having a 37-year old -

Belichick: We're on to Cincinnati. It's nothing about the past, nothing about the future. Right now we're preparing for Cincinnati.

Question: Do you think the talent you have here is good?

Belichick: We're getting ready for Cincinnati.

Question: Do you think you've done enough to help Tom Brady?

Belichick: We're getting ready for Cincinnati. That's what we're doing.

Although the media may not have liked the message, it was clear that Belichick was not going to let the loss be a distraction. As Erik Frenz of Boston.com said, "A press conference is directed at three groups: your players, your owner, and your fans. It seems Belichick's message to those three groups was that the team will not linger on the lumps it took in the 41-14 bloodbath against the Kansas City Chiefs."

At the end of the season, Belichick was asked about the "We're on to Cincinnati" phrase and how it sparked a rallying cry for the Patriots.

"It probably wouldn't have been a big deal if I didn't say it 12 times, or however many times it was," he said in a radio interview. "I couldn't think of anything else to say and it was the same questions that I didn't want to answer."

"I was just trying to move on to really what was important to us at that point, and it was Cincinnati, not Kansas City, and what everybody thought was wrong" with the team.

Belichick understands that his job is not to explain things to the media. His job is to win football games and to put his players in situations where they can do that. Adding fuel to the fire of distractions does not accomplish that goal. He understood that at that moment in time, his number one priority was to focus on Cincinnati. It wasn't time to analyze Tom Brady's age, or if his window for winning was closing. It was to focus on the next game.

Good decisions are not based upon outcomes

Bill Belichick is not afraid to go against the grain. Based on his knowledge and constant learning, Belichick is always innovating on the field to gain a competitive edge. However, sometimes his innovative ways may not get the results that he wants.

The most famous example of a Belichick gamble that didn't work out took place in November 2009, when the Patriots faced the Indianapolis Colts.

With 2:08 seconds remaining, the Patriots were leading by 34-28 and were facing a 4th and 2 on their own 28 yard line. The Colts only had one timeout remaining, so if the Patriots picked up the first down, then the game was over. However, if they failed to pick up the first down, the Colts would have the ball inside the 30. Thus, the more conventional play would have been to punt the ball, pushing the Colts back about 50 yards.

Belichick decided to go for it on 4th and 2. The book *Scorecasting*, written by Tobias Moskowitz, a Finance Professor at the University of Chicago, and L. Jon Wertheim, a writer from Sports Illustrated, explains why going for it on 4th and 2 was statistically the right call.

According to the authors, an average NFL team converts on a fourth and two about 60 percent of the time. If the Patriots failed to convert, the chances of the Patriots still winning despite the Colts having the ball inside the 30 would still be at 67 percent. What that means is that the Indianapolis Colts had a One in Three chance of scoring a touchdown within two minutes from inside the 30 yard line.

If the Patriots punted the ball, an average punt would have given the Colts the ball at their own 30 yard line. From that distance, the Patriots would then have a 79 percent chance of winning. That means that punting would only increase the Patriots chances of winning by 12 percent. If you include the fact that the Patriots had a 60 percent chance to basically win the game by going for it on 4th and 2, then going for it was the better decision.

"Adding everything up, going for it gave the Patriots an 81 percent chance to win the game versus a 72 percent chance if they punted. Even tweaking these numbers by using different assumptions, you'd be hard pressed to favor punting," the authors wrote.

The Patriots had a better chance to win the game by going for it on 4th down. However, the worst possible outcome happened instead. The Patriots failed to convert on the fourth down, and the Colts were able to score a touchdown and won the game 35-34.

Here are some of the quotes by the media and football analysts after the game:

- "You have got to play the percentages and punt the ball."-Tony Dungy, Former Head Coach of the Indianapolis Colts and NBC Football Analyst.

- "I hated the call. It smacked of 'I'm-smarter-than-they-are' hubris. This felt too cheap." -Peter King, Sports Illustrated.

- "My vocabulary is not big enough to describe the insanity of this decision," - ESPN Analyst and Former NFL Quarterback Trent Dilfer.

As Moskowitz and Wertheim write, "Of course none of these criticisms mentioned that punting was statistically inferior or at best a close call relative to going for it. In fact, the claimed the opposite, that punting was the superior strategy. It wasn't."

Despite the heavy criticism for what was essentially the right call, Belichick did not let the negative outcome affect his decision making process. In fact, the very next week, the Patriots faced a 4th and 1 on their own 38 yard line. Instead of punting, the Patriots decided to go for it again. This time, they got the first down.

Belichick didn't let the outcome of the Colts game affect him or cause him to change his strategy. He understood that the DECISION to go for it on 4th and 2 was the right decision. Even though he failed to get the first down, it was still the right decision. He didn't let the OUTCOME change his thinking.

This style of thinking is used by other professionals, such as Wall Street traders, investment bankers, even poker players and gamblers. There are times when the outcome simply doesn't work out in your favor. Sometimes you can't control the outcome. But you can control the decision making process. If it was the right decision to make, then don't let a negative outcome change your thinking.

Adaptability

A key reason why the New England Patriots have been able to win over the course of 15 years is due to the ability of Belichick to adjust to the environment.

As previously mentioned, Belichick has a strong knowledge of the history of football. Based on his education, Belichick is able to understand the flow of the game, the underlying strategy, and the evolving nature of the game. This knowledge gives him the ability to quickly see changes in the game.

"The biggest thing I feel that if you know the history of the game, you understand that it's a changing game," Belichick told CBS This Morning. "There's a lot of evolution to it."

The understanding that the game is always changing gives Belichick the comfort in knowing that he can change his strategy at any time. He isn't afraid or held prisoner to a certain way of doing things because he knows that change is constant.

When he won his first Super Bowl in 2001, "There were no (or few) read options quarterbacks in the NFL in 2001." writes Dan Wetzel of Yahoo Sports. "There weren't really any spread offenses. Defenders used to be able to maul receivers. A franchise running back was highly valued. Coaches talked about controlling the clock, not forcing tempo."

The tempo of a game is a clear example of how quickly and efficiently Belichick can adjust his team to the current environment. The tempo and speed of a game can be determined by the number of plays an offense runs during a game. The faster and quicker a team plays, then the number of plays that they run in a given game will be higher.

Back in 2010, the Patriots averaged 62.6 plays per game, according to statistics listed on the website teamranking.com. That ranked the Patriots as 21st in the league, a full 5 plays per game behind the leader New Orleans Saints.

After that season, Belichick realized that a faster tempo was becoming a competitive advantage in college. With the fast paced offense of Oregon and other college programs, Belichick spent that offseason talking to various college coaches across the country. He learned the key points and advantages of running the spread offense and putting pressure on the defense with a faster pace.

The results was complete revolution in the way the Patriots ran their offense. By 2012, the Patriots led the league in the number of plays per game with a staggering 74.3 players per game, roughly 12 plays more than they ran just 2 season before.

And it wasn't just more plays, it was the type of plays being called. When he won his first Super Bowl back in 2001, Belichick ran the ball and passed the ball at an equal rate, with the Patriots calling just 9 more pass plays than running plays. In 2012, New England called 118 more passing plays than running plays.

Even being able to adjust his team at the larger, macro level, Belichick is also able to change his team on a weekly basis. Belichick entire strategy of winning games is based upon exploiting and attacking the weakness of his opponent. As KC Joyner wrote in Scientific Football, "Belichick's play-calling is the epitome of the Tony Dungy saying that I have been so fond of quoting over the years, '70% of NFL games are lost rather than won.'"

"Belichick takes this mind-set to heart by always going after the weakness of an opponent," Joyner writes. "It it is a schematic weakness such as an offense always blocking a certain type of blitz the same way, he'll exploit it. If it is a personnel weakness, he'll target that. This is by far and bar none the centerpiece of the Belichick's philosophy of winning games."

An example of this was in the 2012, when the Patriots lead the league in offensive plays and had 118 more passing plays than running plays. When facing the Indianapolis Colts in the playoffs, the Patriots completely changed their offensive strategy. The Patriots felt that they could attack the weak rushing defense of the Colts, so they ran 46 running plays and 25 passing plays. They had 234 rushing yards compared to 185 passing yards. The game plan worked to perfection, as the Patriots scored 6 rushing touchdowns while beating the Colts 43-22.

This fluid strategy of adjusting to the larger trends as well as to the specific opponent is not contained to the offensive side of the ball. After winning his fourth Super Bowl in February 2015, Belichick decided to change up his championship winning defense during the offseason. With no hesitation and no emotional attachment, Belichick spent the offseason leading up to the 2015 season retooling his defense.

"The core tenets of Bill Belichick's football program always will remain the same: Versatility is key. Do your job. Hide your weakness and attack their," writes the Boston Globe. "But Belichick is smart enough to not be rigid in his ways. Even at 63 years old and with four Super Bowl rings on his nightstand, he's constantly seeking out new information and his plan of attack is evolving."

"This time," write the Globe, "he's changing his philosophy on defense - right after winning another Super Bowl, no less."

Flexible Personnel

This constant fluidity in the game plan requires Belichick to have intelligent players who can adjust each week to a new style of play. By bringing in smart football players and combining it with his mental training, Belichick is able to create a smart, fast moving team.

"This has two rewards," writes Joyner in Scientific Football. "First, intelligent players are going to be able to adjust to new game plans. Second, because the game plan is based on the opponent, the plan each week is always going to be a fresh one. This approach will appeal to intelligent players and keep their interest levels higher than it would unintelligent ones. Mental stimulation is an extremely effective tool in helping an organization stay focused late in the year."

However, in order to have flexible players, Belichick also needs coaches who are able to adjust. Belichick trains his coaching staff to be able to coach both sides of the ball and to be able to move where needed. As Seth Wickersham and KC Joyner wrote in ESPN, Belichick "cross-trains his coaching assistants."

"The more diverse a young coach's experience the more he understands how Belichick works, and the closer he is to teaching Belichick something the head coach doesn't know," they write.

So former coach Josh McDaniels worked on defense and scouting before becoming the quarterbacks coach, while Eric Mangini worked on the offensive side before moving to the defense. Belichick himself says that by moving coaches around, "they get how our system fits together."

Tailored Strategy

This ability to change strategies quickly is one of the main reasons for his competitive advantage. Chris Ryan of Grantland writes that Belichick has become one of the greatest coaches in football history because he is able to adjust each gameplan to the opponent that week.

"Unlike the many coaches who identify with a particular style or tree, Belichick isn't locked into a singular ideology," writes Ryan. "He seems to effortlessly shift between tactics from week to week, and he's always bristled at attempts to neatly characterize his defenses, once calling the notion that he prefers a 3-4 defense a 'media fabrication'."

In the mind of Belichick, there is no set way of accomplishing your goal. There is no grand idea that must always be followed in order to achieve results. "For Belichick, there are no pure defensive systems, only objectives and constraints and a hyperrational evaluation of each," Ryan writes.

This is how Belichick himself explains his decision-making process on defense: "You decide defensively how you want to defend them in the running game. Do you want to defend them with gap control? Do you want to two-gap? Do you want to try to overload the box with extra guys and play eight against seven or seven against six? Those are all the choices you make," Belichick is quoted as saying.

"With every decision, there's going to be an upside, there's going to be a downside. There will be advantages to playing certain things, there will be disadvantages," Belichick says while sounding like a Wall Street trader.

That seems to be the underlying mindset of Bill Belichick. There is no right strategy that can be applied to every situation. Each game, each season is a new entity, and trying to force what worked in the past will simply not work.

"Thanks to that mentality, Belichick's greatness has never stemmed from the Big Idea," writes Chris Ryan in Grantland, "unless the Big Idea is the relentless application of many Little Ideas."

Review Questions

1. How do you deal with distractions? Although you may think you are addressing it, are there times when you are contributing to the distractions? Are you giving your organization the ability to focus on their roles and eliminating the noise?

2. How are you judging your decisions? If you make a decision and the outcome isn't favorable, was the decision-making process flawed? How do you come to your decisions? If you change the way you come to your decisions, then the results will eventually change as well.

3. How are you adapting to your environment? Are you embracing changes in your workforce? Are you afraid to change what's working? Belichick changed his defense after winning the Super Bowl. Do you have that type of ability to change the way you are doing things?

Keys to Success

1. Clearly define the roles of everyone in the organization.

2. Hold people accountable for their roles, and help them when they accept responsibility.

3. The most vocal person isn't necessary the leader. Be on the lookout for people who are doing their job well in a quiet manner.

4. Improvement takes place on a daily basis. It happens at practice, at training sessions, and in doing your job on a day-to-day basis.

5. You must take the time to learn about the larger trends in your industry.

6. The goal is to "move the football", not prove that your way of doing things is the right way.

7. Use any source that can help you gain an advantage. Whether its statistics, technology, or individuals,, don't hesitate to gain valuable information from a source.

8. Your strategy must be tailored to your current situation. What worked in one situation will not necessary work in another situation.

9. Focus on the task at hand. Don't get caught up in any distractions, and don't contribute to any distractions. Know what you job is, and don't stray from it.

10. Control what you can. You can control your effort and your decision-making process. You cannot control results and outcomes.

About Leadership Case Studies

Leadership Case Studies provides brief reports and analysis on successful individuals. We focus on the habits, strategies, and mindsets of high-performing people in the sports, business, and entertainment industries.

Links to the case studies articles, videos and speeches are all listed on the website.

Started in July 2015, Leadership Case Studies released its first case study on University of Alabama Football Coach Nick Saban, winner of 4 national championships.

Website:
http://www.leadershipcasestudies.com

Additional Leadership Case Studies

The Management Ideas of Nick Saban

The Turnaround Strategies of Jim Harbaugh

The Motivational Techniques of Urban Meyer

The Leadership Lessons of Gregg Popovich

The Work Ethic of Tom Brady, Peyton Manning, and Aaron Rodgers

The Team Building Strategies of Steve Kerr

68384711R00029

Made in the USA
San Bernardino, CA
03 February 2018